# PROGRESSING

# WITHIN AN

# ORGANIZATION

# Progressing Within an Organization:

*Removing the Barriers to Meaningful Progress at Work and Beyond*

By Joel J. Marquardt

ISBN: 9781705893777

Dedicated to,

*"Human beings utilizing the courage to increasingly witness his or her own perceptual tendencies."*

# Contents

# Context

My attempt to survive and thrive within manufacturing organizations for more than twenty-five years has been a journey regularly fluctuating from all-consuming suffering to profound peace with exponential career progress. My involvement in nonprofit, community development, and academic organizations has shown me that no matter what type of organization you immerse yourself in, you are subject to human nature, groups of people influencing each other, and the challenge of seeing functional situations from the most productive viewpoints.

My path from unskilled labor to skilled technical positions required functional expertise along with business acumen to progress from entry-level supervision roles to management to executive. All of this accumulated knowledge—though required to propel my career forward—was hardly the beginning of what has been vital to working with hundreds or thousands of fellow employees and the constantly shifting influences on initiatives. The challenge—at times seemingly impossible—has been to identify and remove barriers by which the vast majority of people limit their progress within their organization or even struggle to sustain a current position.

So many incredibly wise mentors across disciplines—along with endless transformational books and audios—over the decades have challenged me to discover and remove numerous barriers. Hundreds of wonderful human beings have partnered with me across organizations to systematically experiment with distilling effective approaches for improving organizational culture and financial performance among other contributions. Such improvements are accomplished by people unearthing their barriers and removing them. The following reflections briefly summarize some of the most vital content; each point is not complete on its own but is intended to stimulate contemplation for you to manifest your optimal progress, which will emerge through the process of wrestling with the material.

# How to Utilize This Format

Given the intensity of most people's lives, this material is intended to be concise. Therefore, it may require a bit of focus to read each carefully chosen word. The examples included are not of any specific individuals (any resemblance to actual people is only coincidental); rather, they are archetypes that repeat to differing degrees, which were personally experienced across various organizations I was employed in. This material is intentionally not about my specific journey or me. The style is more like a reporter writing an article based on observations.

People have found this resource valuable as a reference book and as a catalyst to simply stimulate contemplation, which leads to the generation of unique solutions. The points are independent and useful out of order, though it may be beneficial to read all of them prior to exploring in random order. Some people find value in the statements of each primary point by simply reading them in the table of contents. In the text, each point is unpacked in the first paragraph following the point heading. This is followed by one paragraph with an example of failure and then one paragraph with an example of progressing as a result of utilizing the spirit of the particular approach.

# 1.

# Facilitate Progress Rather Than Providing Rigid Answers

We typically begin a position within an organization with aspirations to make a difference and to progress. We usually bring strong opinions or create them over a few months, though we are not fully aware we are doing so. We will be expected to contribute sooner rather than later, so we cannot simply observe for an extended period. It is critical we identify the concepts and opinions we have formed or are automatically forming to enable ourselves to suspend them. From an investigator's orientation, we need to explore the territory objectively with its countless unique variables relative to people and processes. Optimal results are derived from facilitating progress that is possible given the existing system rather than forcing approaches from other organizations or conceptualizations we envision that are not completely connected with the subtle, specific circumstances presently in place.

One of the more extreme examples of someone starting a new job and thinking they already had all the answers involved a person managing a plant of over one hundred people. He'd had a long career with another company that had grown from a tiny manufacturer to a national household name—the company had sent him to set up plants around the country and had celebrated his success. He joined a new manufacturer in another industry and began converting it to run exactly as his previous organization had. Within a few months, the plant lost the majority of its profits and was continuing to drop before he was quickly terminated. Several leaders spent many hours every week desperately attempting to assist him in seeing that his new manufacturing circumstances were actually the opposite of those in his previous industry—a fact that he was not willing to permit himself to see at all. Even more painful than the financial catastrophe, his arrogance alienated many leaders who had already taken the plant to above-average performance prior to his interference.

Another individual with extensive training and experience implementing world-class manufacturing techniques faced similar circumstances when entering an organization—he had actually taught classes on his manufacturing approaches and was very passionate about them. Within a few months of being immersed in a different industry, he was able to realize the approaches that had been the foundation for success in other industries would actually put his new organization out of business. He spent long hours observing the reality of the current team of people and business functions and then designed numerous exercises to experiment with options to facilitate the progress of this unique situation. His ability to surrender his assumptions and mental models to navigate unknown territory resulted in doubling profits, which only continued to improve substantially and in a sustainable way. The team leaders enjoyed the precious journey of increasingly identifying and testing perspectives, yielding unexpected progress in organizational performance as well as in their personal lives.

# 2.

# Seek an Understanding of the Organization's Unique Identity

Similar to the uniqueness of every person or family, each organization has evolved from innumerable influences as it has grown and been conditioned. If it is more than a few years old, and especially if it has existed for decades, likely many different leadership approaches have occurred along with shifting external factors. In an organization with many employees, each employee has a significant amount of behavioral tendencies that affect how things are done. The organization exists to benefit those it serves, and comprehensively outlining the reasons for its current effectiveness can be rather elusive. Often people join an organization and push for it to change so they or their role may function better without considering the context they are in and its relative relation to the effectiveness of the entire organization and all stakeholders. There are reasons why everything is the way it currently is, and sustainable progress requires evolving the deeper landscape—not imposing solutions that are not compatible.

After more than a decade with an internationally known brand, a person responsible for tens of millions in annual business activity joined a different organization. She enthusiastically attempted to influence her new organization with the processes and philosophies that had proven foundational for her previous company's success. As it became clear her dozens of initiatives were generating no financial results and increasingly limiting the performance of her team, several leaders attempted weekly to help her see the unique circumstances of her current organization. She was asked to leave after many more months of insisting ways her new organization should be like her previous one—everything would be fine if everyone and everything would change to the way she felt it should be— rather than engaging in dialogue with respect to the landscape of the unique business circumstances she now found herself in. A highly talented, smart, and driven person was rendered completely ineffective as a result of not being able to permit herself to make the subtle shift to perceive and work with her new reality rather than the past mental conceptions she clung to.

In another situation, an individual joined an organization in a position that was created with the sole purpose of implementing world-class manufacturing approaches within the exact same business scope described in the previous paragraph. His diverse education and experience was superior in this field. Initially he attempted to lead major initiatives in the same way as he had previously done in other organizations. Without intervening executives coaching him—even against their direction—he had the courage to observe the ineffectiveness of his approaches and intuitively began to discern the differing circumstances he found himself in. He then generated systems and teams unique to his new organization as he facilitated the continued exploration of solutions across the organization for its dynamic situations. The result was increasing net profit by millions of dollars annually for more than the dozen years he was there.

# 3.

# Hold the Inherent Value of Each Person

All people have done their best to navigate innumerable influences throughout their journey, such as social culture, family, education, employment, and media. More often than not, those we encounter are currently working through significant life challenges in one or more areas. Interacting with people through the lens of this perspective does not mean permitting dysfunction to continue. Continue to progress, and assist others in doing so. This may mean moving in the opposite direction of a person with unproductive tendencies, but take action with compassion and without needing to make the other person appear wrong or inferior.

A member of an organization's management team had risen to management in a previous organization that ended in failure. He again advanced personally in his new organization because of his strong work ethic and sharp intellect. Within months of him reaching the height of his career success, significant responsibilities were taken away from him several times. The primary reason was not that he did not care what people thought, but that he truly could not or would not care about most people in the organization and see them as human beings. He operated from a perspective that all people around him were actually inferior.

An example of the opposite orientation was an individual who entered an organization and authentically tried to settle into a position without any interest in seeking promotion. This individual genuinely saw the preciousness in each employee. He consistently shared developmental information he had been fortunate enough to have been exposed to with anyone interested without forcing it. Year after year, the organization pushed more departments on this person, many of the managers stating they would like to report to him. He humbly would push back each time and not accept the formal organizational chart changes for months before acquiescing. The subtle distinction is that this person—though he had almost no social interactions and was not even a friendly person—was simply committed to enriching the capacities of others. He disciplined and terminated more employees than had previously been done, but the hundreds of employees in the organization somehow did not generally view him negatively. This was possible because the terminated employees were absolutely not seen as inferior but rather just viewed as not being fits for the organization type—some even continued a highly regarded connection with him after termination.

# 4.

# Explore the Broader Context of Situations

If something does not make sense or you detect energy that is less than neutral, there are variables—or an interconnectedness—you are not aware of. It is impossible to know every bit of context, and it is typically not worth investigating. However, for extreme challenges or those that are continuously limiting, it is worth pausing. Attempt to contemplate the circumstances from a resting state while holding the situation out away from you, putting space around it. Set your intention to genuinely perceive the situation comprehensively and from different angles—as well as to observe them as they are rather than how you think they are or wish they were. The value is in shifting away from strictly mental processing of known information to more of an intuitive awareness of the aspects not fully known or knowable—a different kind of perceiving rather than a different degree of the same type. Engaging with others may assist us in becoming unstuck in our perspective as long as the people you connect with facilitate exploring alternate considerations rather than affirming your current understanding.

A rather extreme example of struggling to employ the above was a manager of dozens of people. He physically demonstrated being consumed with frustration almost daily. He remained in his position for years; several leaders attempted to help him become more productive and enjoy his day a little more. He was aware of his tendencies to some degree and did improve some; but he continued to default to viewing things from a very narrow perspective—only recognizing parts of the specific content of a situation without being open to understanding more of the broader context. He would debate endlessly and attempt to bring others into insignificant specific content that would have no substantial impact even if perfected, while becoming an increasing barrier for other departments within the context of the entire organization. He was ultimately terminated from his position—resulting in substantially increased productivity in the organization and far less psychological pain for many throughout various departments.

In another case, a manager with a similar position more often than not perceived situations from the context involved as he took action on the specific content requiring activity. He could be faced with circumstances that were less than ideal and choose options that resulted in the best performance and culture of the entire organization for years to come—rather than being limited by trying to make each minor aspect perfect, which would prove unachievable. He still experienced brief irritating thoughts and emotions throughout the week, but he was able to re-orient himself quickly and view the situation objectively. He did acknowledge that he regularly needed assistance from others to keep himself at his best, and he became effective at orchestrating the needed support. This approach resulted in sustained improvement in culture and financial performance, increasing net profits by hundreds of thousands of dollars annually.

# 5.

# Support Progress That is Naturally Attempting to Emerge

M ost progress is pursued by intellectually fabricating a narrative or plan followed by forcing it onto the current organizational landscape. There is a critical role to be played by the intellect, but it is in facilitating and driving progress more organically. Progress, wisdom, and energy are naturally attempting to manifest in the same way a human being's heart beats or plants grow in the forest. Increasing our ability to witness objective reality from a place of stillness permits discovering a possibility that is almost always overlooked. By tuning into this, it is possible to work more productively with the natural flow of a person, group, or set of processes. If initiatives are energy draining, this is evidence of misperceived circumstances; and progress will not occur or be sustained if it does. Energy should be gained in pursuit of particular progress. The subtle difference, though, is that the process is energizing from a neutral place and openness rather than from emotion that fades when things are not going according to our preferences. Utilizing the tendencies, strengths, and energy of the current circumstances—including people and processes—will produce optimal and sustainable results. With this foundation in place, intellectual planning and bringing in external resources will be effective as well.

A member of an organization's management team intensely operated from the hypothetical. He regularly dug in about how he thought a situation should be. He brought in a consultant to force popular techniques in various areas. The consultant—advisor to many well-known organizations—actually stated he felt guilty charging his fee, as his expertise did not apply to the circumstances at hand. The manager demanded the work continue; he just could not hear the feedback from the consultant and deeply believed all processes and people involved in the currently profitable situation were inferior and could not be built upon. After months of maddening, energy-draining activity regarding these failing initiatives, the management person was forced to leave the organization.

In another organization, a leader invested much more money, paying consultants to teach management the exact techniques referenced in the above paragraph. However, this leader very deliberately constructed context before, during, and after the consultants' coaching with respect to how to use the spirit of the training to apply it appropriately to his organization's unique dynamics. The orientation was to contemplate alternative approaches to the current reality rather than to eradicate it. The subtle difference was that the leader in the second scenario inspired the existing hundreds of people along with their processes to implement thousands of improvements over the following years. The generative energy could be felt as the organization increased its profits by millions annually. A dozen of the primary leaders each went on to dramatic career achievements resulting from their enriched perspectives during this time.

# 6.

# Utilize Inquiry to Enrich Individuals' Capacities

Too often most of us attempt to assist people we know in their development by providing excessive specific advice or by resolving a specific situation. This is appropriate at times. However, the innumerable situations people will find themselves in, beyond a specific incident, remain unaddressed to a large degree. Exploring the perspective the person has and his or her possible approach with open-ended questions uncovers potential options previously not evident. It is critical the questions are in no way attempting to lead them to a predetermined end—this risks them feeling manipulated. They then develop the ability to coach themselves to overcome perceptual or external barriers at any moment. As appropriate, more advanced inquiry may be focused on assisting individuals to increasingly observe their thoughts, emotions, and habits, which will begin to subtly enhance their material progress as well as their quality of life.

Micromanagement was a term used by many to describe a certain manager. He felt the need to critique almost every word from any email of the managers who reported to him. The emails are just an example of how he approached everything in his day. Because of this, he felt he was the best in the organization at mentoring and developing people. His behavior resulted in employees in all positions experiencing paralysis with simple daily activities as they were uncertain how to conduct their functions perfectly and were even fearful of the condescending commentary that might follow from upper management.

After experiencing the environment just described for years, one leader—who had been the abovementioned manager's direct report—conducted herself in a similar orientation as her boss, even though the micromanager ended up no longer working for the company. She continued to reflect on the freedom she was now enjoying reporting to a different person and committed herself to helping people pursue their best lives. Rather than seeking perfection in every detail, she helped people consider the directional value of their efforts. Genuine and heartfelt inquiry became her most valuable asset. Weekly, her skills aided others in navigating some of the most difficult emotional circumstances in conducting business; she helped people work with reality, with all of its positives and negatives. The organization shifted from valuing her for transactional activities with some cultural awareness to regarding her as one of the top two most vital people in the daily organizational functioning with respect to culture and performance—though she still truly did not view herself as this. Many of the most influential leaders in the organization considered her year after year to be the one who most nurtured them in their development, career progress, and happiness.

# 7.
# Identify and Remove Barriers to Progress

As your capability to accurately observe variables—as well as how things are related—evolves, barriers will begin to be more obvious. At times, there is a severe or easily identifiable obstacle that must be removed, or the approach must be altered. Beyond this, the value is in learning to see variables and relationships as a system rather than isolated circumstances. Within a system there are leverage points that can be addressed to permit more progress that is naturally attempting to manifest. The focus shifts from improving a process, person, or team independently to watching the particular organizational system as a whole to find evidence of where important information flows, interactions, or other indicators pointing to performance being limited. It is not that a process, person, or team does not require improvement, but the subtle orientation shift is from perfecting one as a stand-alone function to improvements that will increase the performance of the entire system. Interestingly, optimal organizational performance often requires a localized function to operate a bit less efficiently—which appears illogical and would be altered if an employee was only considering the best practice for the individual function.

A manager was brought into an organization after decades with a national brand. He drove efficiency up, improved his team, and reduced expenses dramatically. Unfortunately, he focused so aggressively on what would be most efficient for the individual functions he was responsible for that he began to negatively impact internal organizational productivity and insufficiently care for customers. The organizational leaders observed that while he was excellent at maximizing the performance of his individual functions, the organizational system was increasingly suffering. He was coached weekly for years by several leaders and just would not entertain the context of what was best for the entire organization rather than most efficient for his area—resulting in his termination.

From the opposite orientation, a management person consistently viewed situations from the context of the customers, internal departments, vendors, and all stakeholders—the system of people and processes. She would generally ponder aloud—with sincere curiosity, rather than answers—what the impact would be on stakeholders, people around her were not considering. While always striving for ways to operate her team more efficiently, she never hesitated to sacrifice this a bit for the greater good. Although she wanted to avoid hurting anyone's feelings at all costs, she was consistently able to perceive areas in the organizational system that contained barriers, and she even coached a few members of her team to transition out of the organization when it was obvious they were oriented against the unique flow of that organization. Over the years, much of the organization's management increasingly sought her input daily to wrestle with business complexities. She generally enjoyed her position, was compensated well, held significant influence, was highly regarded, and weathered the corporate storms over the years with relative ease—while indirectly significantly contributing to a superior culture and financial performance.

# 8.

# Facilitate Individuals Operating from Their Part in the Larger System

In most cases individuals or departments are more effective for the entire organization when not functioning completely independently or in isolation. Collaboration can be vital for improved effectiveness as employees then understand and consider more of the context of the organizational system as a whole; increased commitment may also result when genuine collaboration is achieved. Often those involved in the collaboration still identify almost completely with their organizational position. When an employee authentically facilitates the exploration and outlines the organizational system and subsystems as well the important role of each person, group, or process, individuals' self-identification begins to shift toward an integrated part of something bigger than themselves or their own position. It is important for employees to regularly wrestle with the aspects of the system from different viewpoints and especially to consider less obvious ways that everything is interconnected. When an individual understands the bigger picture, they are more likely to step outside of their box to serve and participate in beneficial ways. The generative energy, creativity, and conviction often resulting from serving is so much deeper and more powerful than the buy-in of collaborating in a mechanical sort of way. As each person is increasingly able to function from this integrated perspective and contribute toward the integrated whole, typically their inspiration builds, and the organizational culture becomes more meaningful as performance also improves.

An individual was hired onto the management team of a company. He was always positive, energetic, and professional. His team and peers came to strongly resent him as time went on, though, due to his excessive use of collaborative language while always attempting to make himself the hero and have all the answers. Although he typically spoke as though he was considering business functions outside of his own bubble, consistent evidence made it clear he was incapable of actually doing so. Although he was coached regarding his tendencies, the increasing dysfunction and financial losses resulted in his termination.

Within the scope of similar responsibilities, a different individual was a strong performer who worked well independently. He did not portray himself as a collaborator at all, but he always approached daily business decisions from an orientation of how all stakeholders would be impacted. The way he would explain the other variables in the system around a specific business situation was from a place of respect and sharing rather than being condescending or divisive. He continuously pursued understanding for himself and others of the circumstances at hand as he took action; he based his actions on reality rather than his opinions or personal agenda. Creative options from many engaged people continued to emerge over the years with a sense of life-giving energy others would ponder. Promotions were forced on him repeatedly as he continued to demonstrate a remarkable capability to earn and sustain the respect of people across all business functions—resulting in improved performance and culture.

# 9.

# Orchestrate the Progress of Each Function

While positions in an organization are typically assessed in various ways throughout the year, too often the focus is on the position in isolation or on perfecting irrelevant details. Bosses also fall into the pattern of attempting to force positions under their leadership to conduct themselves exactly as they would. This limits the person in such a position from improving through differing approaches. In addition, those in the positions do not experience everything exactly like the boss, which may limit effectiveness. Optimal position definition requires beginning from an orientation of how the position exists within subsystems within the organization—the entire organization—and external stakeholders. Awareness must be maintained that each activity is to support the performance and contributions of the organization, not to pursue aspects that are personal preferences or hypothetical applications. Ideally, positions are outlined in a way that promotes evolving effectiveness over the years rather than adhering to a static definition.

A particularly rigid manager came into an organization in a position that was a significant advancement for him. Pursuing perfection may have done well for him as an individual performer—given his role—but this orientation was catastrophic for success in his new position, and it influenced his team and the organization. His rather bold ambition over the years was to build a powerful empire in a department that was not even a profit center. He actually believed the success of his team was to increasingly halt the output of the primary parts of the organization providing value to its customers rather than assist in enhancing the value provided to them. Although he was coached for years, the hundreds of thousands in profits lost annually as a result of his perspectives and the negative psychological impact on many people resulted in the loss of his job.

An example of a far more productive way to navigate similar circumstances is a person who reluctantly became the manager of a team. She operated with a focus on the requirements of positions under her influence—beginning with the strict expectations and then interpreting and applying them on a case by case basis in an effort to serve the customers and promote internal productivity. She earned respect for her approach of not forcing her power over the years from several of the most influential people in the organization. She continued to shift her inherited team of direct reports toward the same orientation she contributed from. Significantly increased profitability and improved collaboration consistently manifested from her discernment of which details were important; most were considered irrelevant as she was always looking to build more value for all with her input.

# 10.
# Evaluate Team Members' System Impact

It is challenging to build a team without intentionally—or unintentionally—favoring the people we like or those with similar personalities. Even if this is overcome, there is often a tendency to view individuals' effectiveness based on how they achieve individual expectations we place on them—this simply implies their skill in pleasing the person who has authority over them. Optimal organizational results require our primary consideration to be the evidence of how an employee functions within the system of the entire organization as well as with external stakeholders. In other words, team members' effectiveness—relative to their organizational position—is determined by whether progress or barriers are generally occurring around them. Obviously, this does not mean continuing with people who operate without integrity just because they are believed to be good at what they do. This perspective is therefore not personal but is based objectively on what will promote and sustain the progress of the whole.

Over many years, far below average financial performance and violated leaders were the result of one manager's tendencies. He viewed each person based on how he or she made him feel during interactions. He aggressively demanded and prescribed how people should alter their style of interacting with him. The result was dozens of key positions in the organization being occupied by unqualified people whose primary skill set was acting the way the boss liked. Though he would state that this was not how teams should be built, he was unable to perceive this about himself—even though the behaviors were extreme and clear. He also pronounced judgement on everything done or said as absolutely right or wrong. The substandard results persisted for a long time as the status quo continued.

Another manager with an opposite orientation experienced similar responsibilities as the person described in the preceding paragraph. Over the course of many years, this leader intentionally worked on basing his decisions on observing evidence in a particular system to address people who were consistently holding back progress. The challenge was to acknowledge the negative impact consistently surrounding an individual even though coaching sessions individually proved to be fine. He still preferred interactions with certain team members, but he ultimately needed to remove some of them from their positions—though they were good human beings—because of their inability to overcome regularly having a significant restraining impact on many people and functions across the organization. Without fail, this approach yielded above-average financial performance that had not previously occurred within this organization over many decades. He also curated a more humanistic quality of cultural experience across many teams and several different organizations over a career spanning thirty years up that point.

# 11.
# Become Increasingly Able
# to Observe Oneself

Every person has been conditioned by countless influences throughout life; every moment of every day has added to a narrative of how life is believed to function. Each additional input is then interpreted through complex filters of previously constructed mental models. By definition, our narratives will continuously create similar circumstances in our lives as we make choices from previous conditioning. It is easy to feel progress is being made when we overcome a particular obstacle, but when we reflect on each of our journeys over the past few years, many of us feel that evidence of substantial progress is lacking. Moving past repeating patterns requires identifying the general motivations we continuously pursue. When we become still and present, we are able to begin to glimpse our general energy with its degree of positive or negative pull. Witnessing the foundational energy sensation we experience permits us to potentially shift the type of energy or, at a minimum, the way we generate our options—simply becoming consciously aware stimulates alternatives.

A person in one organization was consumed with driving everything to perfection. This orientation did result in above-average personal career achievements for a while, though he did not enjoy life. He also often effectively collaborated with others to achieve superior results. However, when a challenge occurred, he overcorrected in his response—costing the organization hundreds of thousands in profits. He then verbally attacked those he was collaborating with and lost his job as a result. While attempting to retain his position, he argued that he should have worded his approaches differently along with other superficial corrections. He ultimately would not look deeper to understand his consuming, unrealistic expectations for perfection had not been healthy for himself, others, and the organization prior to this event and would not be in the future. In addition to the devastation in his career, he also lost his closest friend.

Another individual was also impossibly demanding of himself and others. Episodes of intense anger were part of his typical daily pattern, and his job was on the line. He found the courage to observe the simmering negative energy he was experiencing regularly. Noticing this negative energy and pondering how his general responses resulting from ordinary work experience could be altered, he became willing to work with himself and his human imperfections as well as the reality of the strengths and weaknesses of others. Over the following years, he came to be known for his harmonious nature and respected job performance as he also shed unhealthy physical habits, losing half his body weight to realize his healthy body state—and keeping it off.

# 12.

# Investigate Critical Thoughts, Emotions, and Activities

It is impossible to endlessly wrestle with every thought, emotion, or physical habit we experience, and this would not actually be beneficial. Identifying the most significant or regularly encountered automatic tendencies we have can have a substantial impact on our progress, though. This applies to less neutral circumstances but also to those that are going relatively well. It is not that we are usually incorrect in our current perspectives, but our perspectives are always limited with respect to the entire context. Even with the understanding of more context, we may still make the same choices but with increased understanding and reduced stress, resulting in potential for more or different progress to emerge. For a moment, attempt to transcend more rigid or certain positionality and mental commenting to promote experiencing the objective reality rather than stories we have regarding it. The most effective inquiry is focused on general tendencies rather than each specific aspect, such as the inability to embrace the uncertainty and ambiguousness of many life situations which results in limited ways of coping with this sensation.

Unfortunately, an extreme example of the destructive results of not having the capacity to investigate one's own thoughts, emotions, and activities was a person in a supervisory role. He was absolutely certain of every opinion he had. A fairly skilled leader attempted to work with him for months to help him improve some of his perspectives in an effort to maintain his position, which was in serious jeopardy when this leader inherited this man and his position. Not only were the opinions rigid, but the employee often demonstrated a physically observable, intense verbal defense of them. Interestingly, he was always certain he had all the information regarding every life situation he encountered, and he was not open to additional facts or data. He was eventually terminated and was consumed with hatred for the leader. He reached out to all the organization's leaders at exactly midnight of New Year's Eve almost a year later in a nasty, retaliatory attempt to hurt the leader who had attempted to coach him. His entire life continued to fall apart over the years after this.

Another individual was known for having rigid positions regarding many circumstances in her life and endless commentary going on in her head. Over the course of several years, she pursued deep, contemplative personal development to create a more enjoyable life. The primary shift was for her to regularly tell herself that maybe something was not as she had perceived it. This subtle loosening of firm attachment is very different than feeling her current view was wrong, researching it more—which can be helpful at times—to alter her opinion, changing her mind, or switching to the opposite position. A lifetime of sleepless nights gradually went away as she gently held most of the same perspectives but without gripping them so tightly. There was an openness around them. Her quality of life transformed far beyond her expectations as her significant career achievements also became a reality with relative ease. Leaders were simply nurtured by her human essence and nonjudgmental, life-giving energy.

# 13.

# Access Wisdom and Life Energy Beneath Thoughts

As your ability to witness your automatic and unique conditioned patterns increases, you'll have more glimpses of your essence beneath the tendencies shared by all humans. Sensing possible approaches more from intuition than intellectual thought permits generative potential for more wisdom and life-giving energy, which is sustainable even after excitement fades or logical perspectives change. The intellectual can then be applied to progress that is more holistic. When you access the more intuitive human capacities, it feels like an alert presence or more of an inner connectedness, a sense of peace, and often subtle joy as we take action. The evidence is that rigid dualism or distinct oppositional opinions begin to soften as we hold all of the perceived good and bad and work with it to manifest a better quality of life as well as, typically, more material achievements. The subtle shift is from being consumed—imprisoned—by the specific content of the moment to perceiving the broader context and dimensions involved. Accessing these capacities can be very elusive.

One individual genuinely pursued significant and diverse development for decades. She used more enlightened words, regularly referenced developmental resources, and truly felt compassionate toward others. However, she could not see that she was continuously finding the next author or model that was the answer for herself and everyone else while aggressively attempting to then convert others as she felt she really was trying to help them. She pursued answers and grasped them with certainty, resulting in her building more mental narratives rather than identifying them and suspending them to access her natural intuitive and holistic solutions. People experienced her as forcing feel-good agendas, given that her compassion evaporated when people perceived things differently than her.

Another individual with a similar developmental path and career responsibilities shared developmental material with people year after year. However, he cautioned people to realize it was always just partially capturing an understanding of the answers that continue to emerge within each human being. He utilized many of the same resources as the abovementioned person to stimulate wrestling with his own limiting mental models and, more importantly, the human mechanism that incessantly creates and then becomes restricted by one's own mental models rather than assuming the material he read had all the answers. This individual completely felt no judgement toward someone who found no value in his perspectives, and he typically only shared material as a result of people seeking him out after experiencing his profoundly healthy response in stressful or uncertain situations. Over the following decades, he repeatedly achieved and sustained career achievements—always in the top couple percent of each organization with which he was involved. More notably, he enjoyed an abundant richness in relationships with those who truly saw him as an average guy on a flawed journey—which had barely begun—to access the precious capacities available to people in life.

# 14.
# Contribute to Progress as an Integral Part of the Whole

Human beings have a deep orientation toward contributing to something—ideally something meaningful to themselves. There is a fulfillment from the activity of creation or manifestation. In addition, it is enlivening when a pathway for progress is detected across the many aspects of one's life journey. A sense of completeness is often experienced when we know we are a vital part of a healthy relationship, initiative, or organization. Discerning ways to add fundamental value for the people and systems we are engaged with will yield optimal sustained performance and satisfaction instead of the brief binge on self-promoting emotions from manipulating others to maximize personal success in an isolated situation. Evidence of contributing to the whole looks like a sort of dance with the iterative nature of activities, given the fluidity of most systems over time, rather than unchanging, explicitly defined action items over an extended period.

One manager demonstrated above-average capabilities to improve results in his given field. He was never happy, though, no matter how many achievements he was recognized for. This individual would not broaden his perspective to consider the increased personal success he might obtain from serving the larger organization. Even more unfortunate was his steadfast belief that he absolutely would not be able to enjoy his workday or other parts of his life more—he was older and completely alone; he had been so his entire life, in all parts of his life. With great sadness, his leader had to remove him from the company after years of compassionate coaching as this manager continued to be a significant barrier for the progress that was happening all around him. His extreme, rigid approaches and superior-sounding answers for everything continued until he took his last step off the property.

One of the higher-salary leaders with an upper management title was often evaluated to determine if he was sufficiently qualified or driving enough results to retain his position. As the years went on, with most of his peers being terminated in an extremely aggressive environment, this individual was never seriously in question. He had many weaknesses, but not one of the hundreds of employees had anything negative to say about him as a person. It was evident he consistently did everything he could to contribute to progress anytime and anywhere across the organization without seeking any praise. The most powerful leaders came to deeply respect him as a cherished part of the organization as he continued to be content to just flow with the shifting circumstances and significantly pitch in beyond the duties of his position.

# 15.

# Provide Nonjudgmental Space
# for Others

Given human nature's tendencies, substantial progress requires potential that emerges from a safe space. This does not mean condoning or continuing with another's dysfunctionality. Your interactions with others are most beneficial when operating from a neutral perspective to permit as much evolution as possible. Your intention is then impersonal—relative to the identity accumulated over their journey—yet provides a sense of cherishing the human essence beneath their lifetime of conditioning at the level of being. Providing this sense of sanctuary nurtures deep healing and a space to rest a bit, which does not guarantee progress but creates favorable conditions. Engaging a person from more typical orientations results in stimulating automatic resistance mechanisms, which block us in walking alongside the person—psychologically or in spirit—in curious exploration of alternate ways of experiencing the specific circumstances. Questions without clear answers may then be utilized to slightly crack tightly held patterns or mental models that are resulting in suffering or limiting progress materially and in quality of experience. Avoid attempting to control others' journeys, and foster their capacity to shape it themselves. Then partner with them, with respect to their position in their journey, or proceed in a direction not involving them without having to make them appear wrong as you do so.

More often than not, a particular management person could not stop himself from quickly cutting off team members after asking them a question as he always truly felt he had a superior perspective. His body language usually conveyed that he judged everything about another person even when he was not verbalizing it. Attempting to be helpful, he would advise those closest to him that intensely controlling everyone and everything was the foundation for success, though this did not result in success for him over the decades to come. He enjoyed not one authentic relationship with the thousands of people he encountered across organizations, and he only received limited and superficial information regarding any organizational situation in which he was involved. People played the artificial role he absolutely demanded while the most capable left him.

Men and women of all ages, from ghettos to more affluent backgrounds, regularly told a different leader how they felt he was just like them or that he was the only one in their life that truly understood them. Hundreds of people over the years truly enhanced their capacities, yielding significant and sustained progress as a result of the nurturing space he often provided. He was a primary part of record organizational performance consistently across organizations. It is critical to understand he was not necessarily a friendly person—he often received feedback that he was intimidating. He also terminated far more people than the average leader in his position from the perspective of the terminated person not being a fit, at least in that part of his or her journey, and never because he or she was a lesser person than he was.

# 16.

# Experience Input from Others Contextually

Often we interpret words or concepts similarly across various people we interact with regardless of the situation. In order to minimize the potential for erroneous or incomplete assumptions, we must maintain awareness that people are sharing from how they experienced the particular circumstances or how they experience most situations, which is not necessarily objectively accurate. Input from another person falls somewhere on the spectrum from completely subjective experience to the opposite side of absolute objective reality. This does not mean we see the person as flawed but simply as human. A significant challenge for us occurs when a person truly believes his or her perspective; we then have a strong tendency to work with the other person's perspective as complete reality. Important interactions warrant identifying or observing contextual evidence to inform our understanding.

A particular manager was extreme in interpreting interactions in a very literal way. It was as though he heard or read each word from another person, looked up one precise definition in the dictionary, and then rigidly clung to this interpretation. He was not willing to consider how current circumstances may be influencing a person's perspective or even the tone of the communication. Often an entire team of peers would agree on an understanding of a situation, but their understanding would be quite different from his. They would compassionately outline it for this manager. He would grip his interpretation even tighter as he supported it with a word or few words from the particular communication along with the textbook definition rather than taking the entire communication—along with the orientation of the person responsible for it—into consideration. This manager was ultimately terminated after years of coaching and costing the organization hundreds of thousands annually.

An example of the opposite extreme was an individual performer who was respected and performed his daily technical tasks well. He was above average with interpersonal interactions for sure, but his most valuable talent was demonstrating an ability to interpret input from another person relative to the circumstances involved, rather than adhering to the literal dictionary definition of the words used. This person would state that another individual had communicated a certain message; then he followed this with additional information. He was remarkable in selecting the relevant contextual influences, such as the kind of day the person was having, the person's general world-view (without judgment), the likely perspectives of someone in that organizational position, personality style, and his or her background, among many other dimensions. Management selected him and progressively promoted him into positions of leadership as he generated a far more enjoyable culture and significantly improved financial performance than the organization had experienced in previous decades. He also more than doubled his income over a few years and continued to experience a sense of deep fulfillment long after.

# 17.
# Discern a Person's Ability to Actually Manifest His or Her Mental Story Line

A regular challenge while interviewing, facilitating projects, or just accomplishing daily transactions occurs in determining whether people are capable of executing a thing they state they can and even believe they are able to. For example, a person genuinely outlining a plan well in a meeting is only demonstrating the skill to articulate something well—possibly even truly enthusiastically—that is also attractive to our intellectual propensities. This is not evidence he or she is capable of actually bringing it to fruition. Interestingly, those who are often superior at the professional and intellectual gymnastics in a meeting often find themselves imprisoned mentally by an endless maze of knowing about things, idealizing, and hypothesizing. It is critical to identify those who are able to navigate the how-to of progress given present circumstances while pursuing optimal progress rather than making decisions based on a person's eloquence or charisma. We then choose our best options for progress while interacting with those caught in idealizing and hypothesizing in a respectful, kind, and more effective way for all.

An inspiring manager was brought into an organization. Right from the start, most felt drawn to her enthusiastic and intelligent thoughts and plans to improve the culture and dramatically improve financial performance. She was a superior exemplar of professional approaches. Her confidence motivated people to collaborate, but few initiatives reached the execution phase as more detail and options were continuously explored month after month. The few action steps that did happen were halted quickly as there was no way to proceed since the elaborate plans were not actually based on the circumstances of the particular company and industry. People felt good during the process for a while but then grew weary, and not one result occurred over an extended period, resulting in her dismissal.

In another case, an individual performer was hired and given the responsibility of managing a new facility and equipment projects, representing millions of dollars of investment. Though not as polished as the preceding example, he was able to speak competently from a foundational business acumen as well as project-specific information. Initially, these two people would appear to be rather similar. However, he did not dominate the conversations and was not as bold when sharing. The primary—though subtle—difference is that he was speaking from the details and context of the present circumstances rather than intellectual narratives that were not actually linked to the current reality. He consistently executed significant activities, resulting in effectively functioning facilities, equipment, materials, and processes that were relatively close to what he described months—or even a year—earlier. Over the years, he enjoyed the results he generated with additional projects and the increasing respect from others while dramatically advancing the company's competencies and saving hundreds of thousands of dollars annually.

# 18.
# Work Nonjudgmentally with All Dimensions Involved

Rigid positionality typically limits or completely restricts progress, at times resulting in a situation disintegrating or deteriorating. Employing nondualistic language has become relatively popular in a sincere attempt to overcome these barriers. While this is usually preferable to operating from a strictly dualistic approach, there is often still an invisible restraint. Pure potential requires the spirit of nondualism at a deeper level. Evidence of lacking this spirit is making the other wrong—often intensely—rather than simply working with our preferred option. This does not mean a particular position will not result in superior results. The subtle difference is whether the energy influencing the situation is generative or inhibiting. Optimal progress occurs when the choice is made while gently holding all dimensions from a neutral to positive orientation.

A member of the management team of an organization intensely judged every aspect of everything he encountered each day. He coped with most things not meeting his expectations by insisting on avoiding them. Everyone in this person's life desperately found ways to minimize interactions with him and to portray the best facade he or she could muster. Interestingly, he regularly emphasized that he did not see things dualistically and insisted others must not—using all the popular language and models. Often, though, he would choose one option, large or small, followed by an all-consuming response making the other options out to be absolutely wrong in every way. He found himself imprisoned by gripping fear and rage, and he was always about to erupt. Unfortunately, this resulted in not one real relationship in his life as well as all competent employees leaving him over time and him foregoing many millions of business profit each year.

Another person with similar responsibilities gradually acquired the ability to work with all of the perceived good and bad of each situation. He knew there were no perfect people or permanently maximized performances—though long-term overall progress is possible and favorable. This manager was comfortable all day, every day, choosing the best option currently available while others did not choose any as they did not believe they had the perfect option, or they made a choice with much negative energy involved. It was not as though he believed his choices were perfect in every way. He did not have to intensely judge each option before making a choice or make people or circumstances out to be wrong in order to make a choice. There was simply fluid action taken from a generally peaceful and energizing space. He found it increasingly easier to consistently achieve substantially higher financial performance for himself and his organizations decade after decade while enjoying each day and numerous relationships of substance.

# 19.

# Staff Positions with People Naturally Oriented Toward the Particular Requisite Essence

Superior performance is typically easier and more enjoyable from deep alignment. Thoroughly contemplate the fundamental nature of a specific position to determine the primary motivation and orientation required to excel. Personality traits are often a good start; then go deeper into what the source of energy would need to be for someone to excel with ease in that position. For example, a position that requires continual expense reduction might be staffed with someone who is always doing this in areas of his or her life prior to being part of the organization. The person then simply takes action from the natural experience of his or her day and can produce superior results; this person may often be confused as to why others struggle in such a position as it seems to be all common sense. Another indicator would be that even if a person's manager placed no value on expense reduction, the person could not help but act from this perspective rather than exclusively from set organizational goals or coaching from a manager.

One person attained several far-above-average positions within organizations, but he was not able to sustain them even though he was a genuinely nice and intelligent person. In one instance, he joined a company and was given the responsibility to reduce expenses for tens of millions spent annually. He came from a family that was fortunate enough to enjoy an upper-middle-class lifestyle for many decades. Given this orientation, he justified all the money spent as being worth it and did not develop any options to reduce expenses over an extended period. In fact, he increased expenses at times because a vendor would make a good point, and the vendors were nice people. His employer experienced him as a regular advocate for each vendor and the status quo rather than for his employer and reduced expenses. While he was not expected to be unfair with vendors at all, he simply could not explore creative ways to collaborate with them to reduce costs for his company and ideally increase profits for the vendor through unique solutions. He was regularly indignant with his employer for coaching him to be more creative, and the company ultimately terminated his employment.

With similar responsibilities, a different person was exceptionally effective, although she had no professional experience or education for such a role. She could not help but to curiously ponder a smarter way to develop her organization's products. While always respectful with vendors, she operated from a conviction that there had to be better options to be found collaboratively. She was able to discern well where there was likely a way to streamline vendor relationships. This individual was able to achieve superior results with no set goals or coaching—she was not trying to achieve something but was just being herself. Performance simply occurred rather than having to identify a facade or techniques and then attempt the hard work of operating from them to achieve success.

# 20.
# Empower Staff as They Demonstrate Competence

A relatively common management challenge is to determine the appropriate level of involvement regarding the staff's execution of responsibilities. There are those who see themselves as superior or needing to control, so they require almost all of each week's activities to be reviewed and adjusted prior to taking action, which can be very stifling unless absolutely necessary. The other extreme is management that avoids almost all details regarding how a direct report is conducting tasks or projects. An ideology of empowerment makes this person feel superior, but substandard performance often results. Optimal performance and job satisfaction is derived from reviewing each type of activity with the appropriate staff member and exploring the most productive approaches together—even searching for external input when warranted. Upon demonstration of successful execution—rather than just talking about it—the direct report then acts independently in future situations within that particular scope. This is repeated with each type of scope and is dynamically maintained over time by working together on items of differing scopes, circumstances with abnormally significant impact, or trending opportunities for improvement.

One management professional would have a weekly review of each activity or project detail with each of the managers reporting into him—even when there was no scheduled new activity on long-term initiatives. His direct reports were deeply disturbed by this ongoing approach and the manager's condescending tone. The lack of motivation was severe as his team was also fearful of taking agreed-upon action without his involvement. Another facet of this tendency was the equal emphasis and time spent on immaterial activities relative to substantial initiatives. In fact, he was often less focused on the most impactful matters. This repetitive waste consumed significant amounts of time weekly as the financial performance did not improve over years and ultimately declined despite long work hours by many.

With similar responsibilities, another manager was known for concentrating his time and interactions on generating new conditions to improve organizational performance. He and each of his leaders began initially in considerable dialogue as they partnered to explore the best approach for each type of activity, though he assumed the responsibility of outlining the ultimate methodology in a way that honored the human dignity of his staff members. As each direct report's achievements and competence was dependably demonstrated, business activities arising daily were only evaluated together under abnormal circumstances. The staff members earned autonomy, resulting in a personal sense of fulfillment along with effectiveness in conducting their functions. Over the years under this man's management, interactions increasingly focused on exploring potential for team members and processes to improve or even experimenting with significantly altered methods. Historic financial performance was consistently improved and sustained.

# 21.
# Enhance Energy in Others through Your Way of Being

An immensely valuable indicator of how effectively and enjoyably you will connect or partner with others emanates from observing the energy flow through interactions. People will attempt to avoid you and remain superficial if you are generally consuming energy from them as a result of bolstering your pride, gaining your desires, or attempting to surmount your fears. Those typically consumed with their own pride, desires, and fears may continue to seek interactions to feed on excitement derived from a preferred circumstance or motivating rhetoric, which unfortunately does not sustain across the daily fluctuations of life. Increasing our capacities to interact with others from a confident humility and resulting compassion while still working with the complete reality of situations—though not favorable at times—works with the energy of life and yields a depth of genuine interaction. Evidence of operating more from this space is that most people will yearn for more interaction and generate progress individually and together.

Overbearing animated greetings and optimistic words set the tone of standard interactions for one particular person. He forcefully taught everyone that this way of carrying oneself and thinking was a superior way to approach life. Those he considered closest to him in life felt they could not be themselves in his presence or share anything real as he demanded they interact in a way that mirrored him. Despite all this humanistic rhetoric, he truly could not entertain anything that did not personally benefit him at that point in his life. This energy limited the financial progress of his career responsibilities substantially over decades as those most competent shut down or left his life.

For decades, when entering any interaction with others, a different individual intentionally witnessed his thoughts and emotions while attempting to suspend them to encounter any person from a neutral place. Though not perfect, he typically was able to experience others without having to make them appear wrong or inferior in any way. This does not mean he condoned dysfunctionality. Progress was always an underlying expectation; while he did not attempt to control it specifically or have to condemn something first, he simply focused on progressing from what the current situation was without the mental or verbal commentary. Many people not directly involved with this person contemplated over the following years how numerous people gained more energy from this person than anyone they had experienced—and he was not trying to motivate anyone in any way. He sustained a journey of increasing material success and quality of life, which was rich in deep, nurturing relationships.

# 22.

# Serve the Highest Good of Others

Too often, a boss operates from the standpoint of consuming a service from an employee. The employee absolutely must adequately contribute to the particular organizational function. However, employees will thrive in performance for the organization if their efforts are an important and integral part of their long-term personal progress. Rather than creating power struggles, authentically supporting your direct reports in enriching their capacities for their career's future, independently of the current organization, actually increases loyalty to you and the organization. Even without the hierarchical relationship, this orientation with others—when sought out, not forced—attracts opportunities and a sense of fulfillment.

Many managers unconsciously believe their staff should be motivated to perform their best simply because the manager is the boss. In some manager's minds, the very definition of the job of a manager is to dictate philosophies and orders in any way they please. A particularly extreme example involved a manager who overtly proclaimed to his direct reports how they were to think and exactly what should inspire them. At his worst, he would cut off his leaders who were expressing an aspiration of others in the organization and decree that he did not care what was important to them and followed by demanding they focus on his desires exclusively. Over many years, he was not able to retain the most competent individuals while those with skill sets that were less marketable remained but in malicious compliance. He was not able to develop and execute successful business initiatives across decades, though he attempted several annually. His staff would become irritated—physically disgusted at times—when summoned to his office to chat about a business situation.

Not one key person left any of another manager's teams that he was responsible for across a couple of organizations over almost twenty years. This manager was often pleasantly surprised to indirectly discover situations where staff went above and beyond without the boss requesting or even being made aware in an attempt for the person to receive praise. The manager reliably approached each day's situations viewing people in the context of increasing their capabilities for their lifelong career journey. He did not permit sustained substandard performance, and he engaged weekly in conversations regarding unfavorable circumstances and terminated many people who simply were not a fit for the type of position or organization—but did so without judging the person as wrong or inferior. His segments of the businesses financially achieved historic results as he did not emphasize that his staff had to perform for him or because the organization deserved it.

# 23.

# Create Conditions for People to Make a Home

Purchasing a house or vehicle often promotes more care taken—as well as numerous improvements—than renting a house or vehicle, in addition to a longer-term inclination. Optimal performance and a more enjoyable workday requires staff to be able to make their position and organization their home. Managers must not manipulate to obtain agreement from others—striving for genuine buy-in is better than not doing so. However, the staff member is still working with your initiative or in your way. The subtle shift from staff viewing their contributions as a service to the boss's home to viewing themselves as creating their own home has a profound impact. Expectations must still exist for manifesting superior results, but the essence of the context is substantially different.

A particular manager regularly and boldly stated that he was the boss to his employees individually as well as in meetings with his team. He felt he was just stating how things really were, and everyone needed to be good with it. Even when not explicitly stating this, it was clear this was his orientation in every interaction. He truly could not and would not consider the way his employees viewed him. Most input was cut off and aggressively challenged. Significant time weekly was required of his managers to attempt to limit the damage from the violation felt by his direct reports and others. Over time—no matter how deep each employee's level of conviction to add value was—the most competent left the team while others put on a facade and performed the bare minimum to survive.

With another manager involved in similar responsibilities as the one outlined in the previous paragraph, each employee was engaged in dialogue with respect to the scope of functional activities required of each position. While this boss definitely had directional, nonnegotiable expectations for outcomes, he genuinely—without rigid opinions—utilized inquiry to explore his perspectives while primarily concentrating on his employee through dialogue in as many sessions as required. The employees were expected to be self-sufficient and were provided real freedom to accomplish the expectations as long as they were respectfully adding value to others and the processes connected to them. Superior results were necessary, though, from the employees as they became sort of their own independent entity as this manager focused on generating value in uncultivated organizational endeavors. None of the most competent staff left his teams across several organizations and decades of consistent historic profitability.

His employees enjoyed precious individual and meaning-ful collective progress.

To connect with the author, email joeljm108@gmail.com.